WELLINGTON SQUARE

The red door

Characters

Rocky Rockwell

Mr Keeping

Ben Harris

Mrs Rockwell

Fred Smith

Scenes

Scene 1 At Rocky's house
Scene 2 In the Square
Scene 3 Back at Rocky's house

Scene 1: At Rocky's house

Outside Rocky's front door. Ben and Rocky are talking and looking at the front door. There is a tin of paint and a brush on the ground.

 **Ben**: What are you doing?
How about playing with the ball in the Square?

 **Rocky**: Not now.
I have to paint the door.
(Rocky bends down and picks up the paint.)
Here is the paint.

 **Ben**: Do you want a hand?
I am good at painting.
I painted my old table.

 **Rocky**: No! I will be quick.
See you later.

 **Ben**: See you later.
(Ben wanders off and Rocky
begins to paint.)

Rocky is painting very quickly and splashing paint all over the wall. Fred and Mr Keeping come by with Bruce.

 **Fred Smith**: What are you doing, Rocky?

(Rocky stops painting and turns to speak to Fred and Mr Keeping.)

 **Rocky**: Painting the door, Fred.
Mum said it looked old and
she wanted it painted red.

 **Mr Keeping**: Well, you have splashed paint on the wall.

 **Fred Smith**: Keep it on the door or your mother will be cross.

 **Rocky**: (sounding a bit cross himself) Yes, Fred.

(Fred walks off.)

 **Mr Keeping**: Do you want a hand?
I am good at painting.
I painted my shed.

 **Rocky**: No, it will not take long.

 **Mr Keeping**: You will have to put on two
coats of paint, you know.

 **Rocky**: (sounding horrified)
Two coats of paint!
That will take all day!

 **Mr Keeping**: (beginning to walk away)
Two coats, Rocky.
Two coats will make it
look good.

 **Rocky**: (muttering to himself)
Two coats will take all day.
I will do one coat.
I want to go and play with Ben.

Scene 2: In the Square

Ben is lying on the ground tossing the ball about.
Rocky is walking over to him.

 **Rocky**: Come on, Ben.
I want to play.
I will be in goal.

 **Ben**: (getting up)
What about the door?

 **Rocky**: (looking pleased with himself)
Painted red like Mum wanted.

 **Ben**: That was quick!

 **Rocky**: Yes. I am good at painting.

(Rocky and Ben begin to play football. Rocky's Mum can be seen coming into the Square.)

 Ben: (kicking the ball past Rocky) Goal! I am in goal now!

 **Rocky's Mum**: Rocky! Rocky! Come here!

 **Ben**: Your Mum looks cross, Rocky.

 **Rocky's Mum**: What did you do to the door?

 **Rocky**: (looking surprised)
Painted it red like you asked.

 **Rocky's Mum:** The door will not open!
You painted the door when it was shut. Now it will not open.

 **Rocky:** I did not know I had to open the door!

 **Rocky's Mum:** You will stop playing and come home.
You will come home and open the door!
(dragging Rocky home)

Scene 3: Back at Rocky's house

Rocky, his Mum and Ben are standing outside the front door. Rocky's Mum is looking cross.

Rocky's Mum: What are we going to do?

Rocky: I know. I will get in through the window.

Ben: I will go with Rocky.
We can pull the door on the inside.

 **Rocky's Mum**: Don't fall!

 **Rocky**: (from inside the house)
We made it!
Now we can open the door!

(Noises can be heard from inside the house as Rocky and Ben pull on the door.)

 **Rocky**: You push, Mum!

 **Rocky**: We did it!
We opened the door.

 **Rocky's Mum**: (looking at her hands)
You opened the door but look at the paint! Look at my hands!

 **Ben**: I am going home now.
See you later, Rocky!
(Ben hurries away.)

Rocky's Mum: I don't want the door looking like that. You will have to paint it again!

Rocky: (looking sulky)
Oh, Mum!

Rocky's Mum: And you can get the paint off the wall!

(Later on that day.)

 **Mr Keeping**: Still painting, Rocky?

 **Rocky**: (sounding fed up)
Yes, Mr Keeping. I am doing two coats like you said.

 **Mr Keeping:** Well, when you have painted the door you can come and paint my fence. See you later!
(Mr Keeping strolls off. Rocky looks really fed up!)